Shops

Interior Design Coloring Book

Shopping Malls, Retail Shops, Grocery Designs Sketches

Rachel Mintz

Images used under license from Shutterstock.com

Join Our Coloring Books VIP Group
Members Get Giveaways, Deep Discount Offers,
Win Prizes – Visit Site To Join (It's Free)

www.ColoringBookHome.com

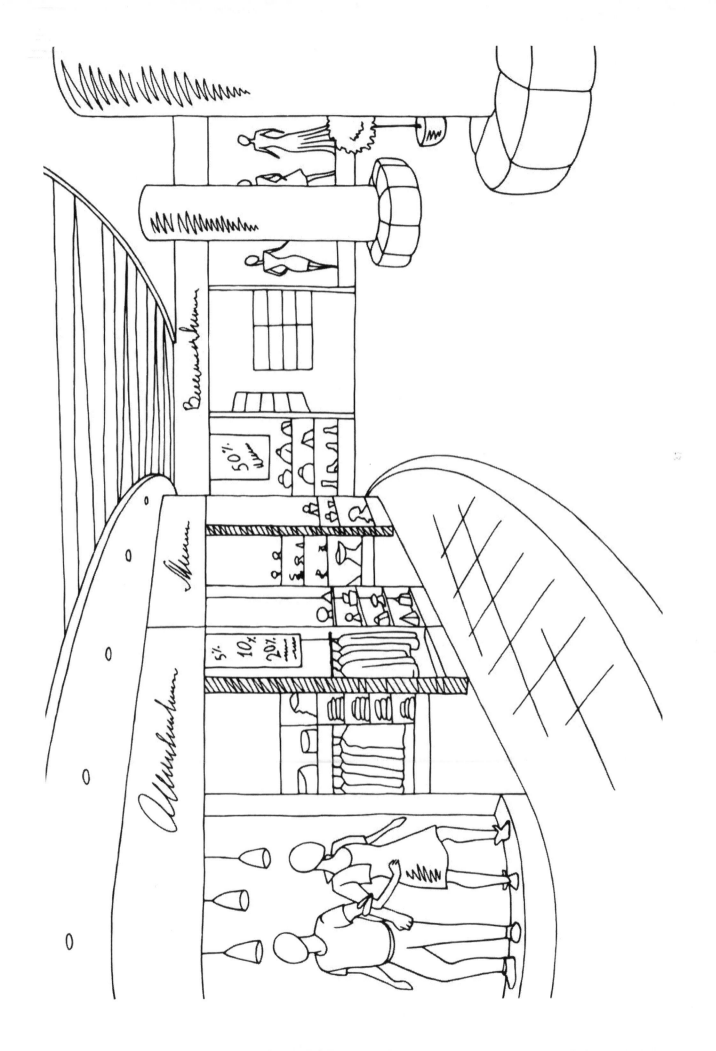

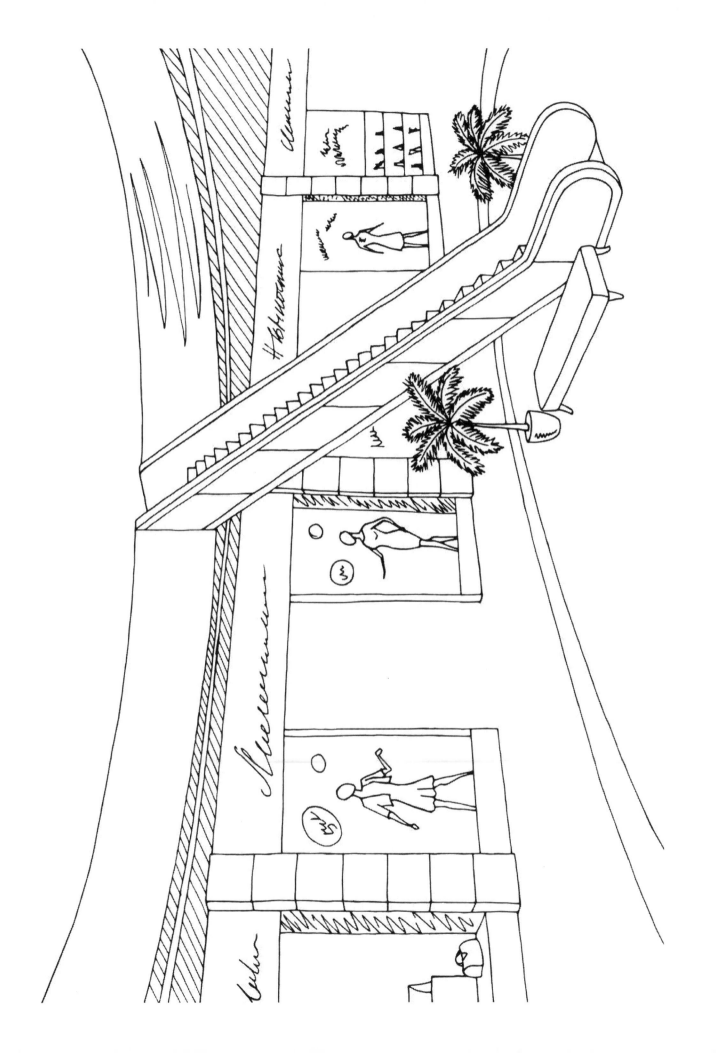

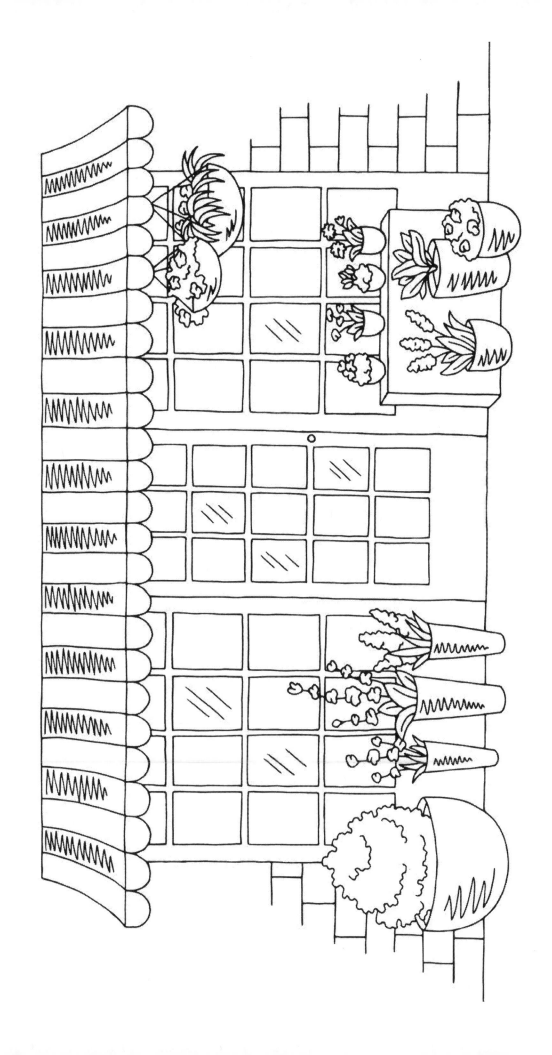

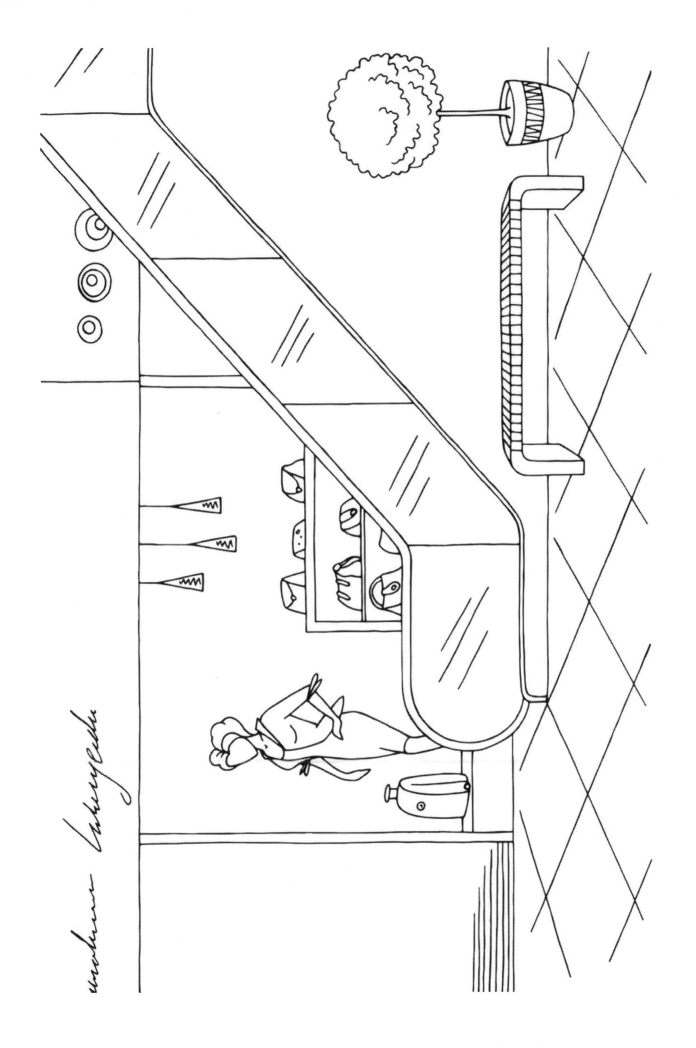

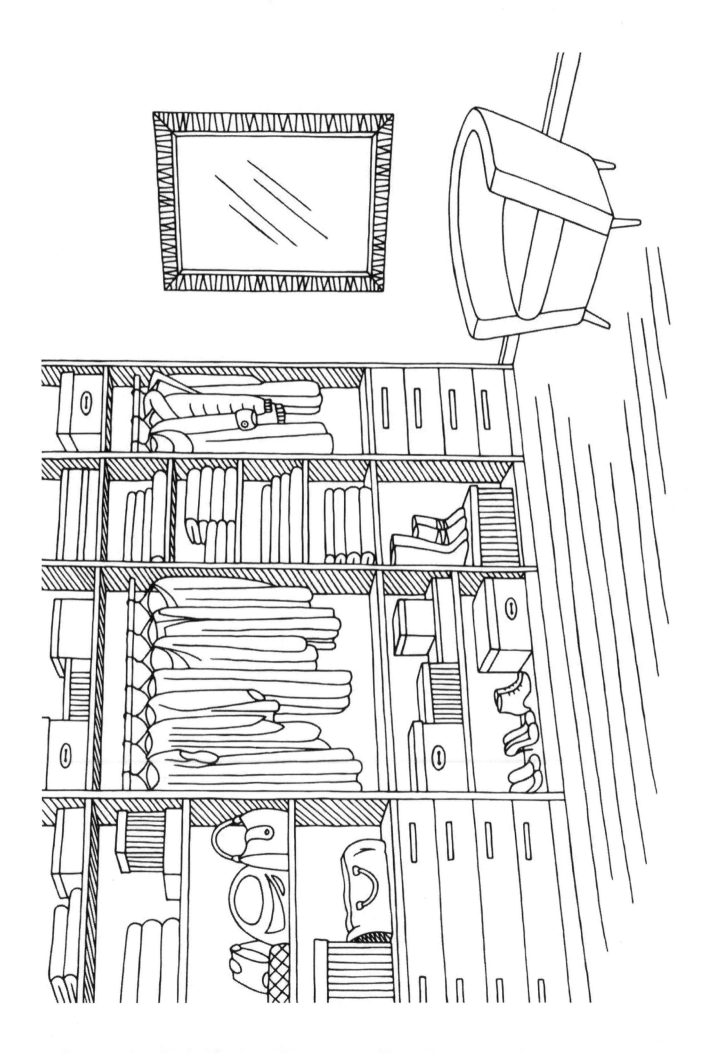

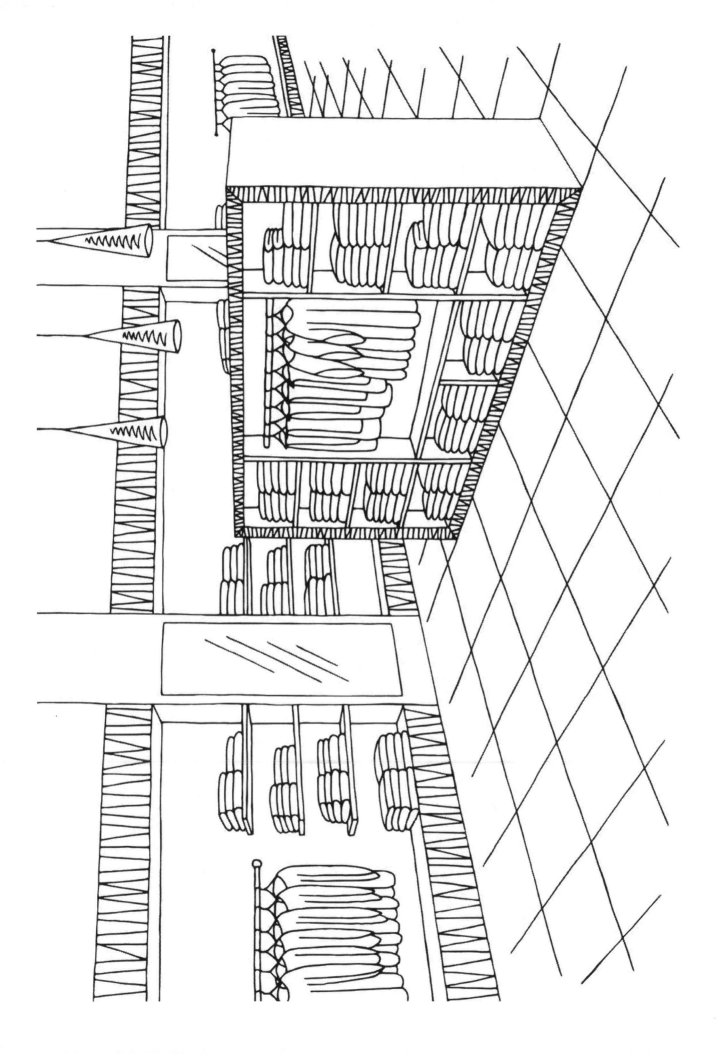

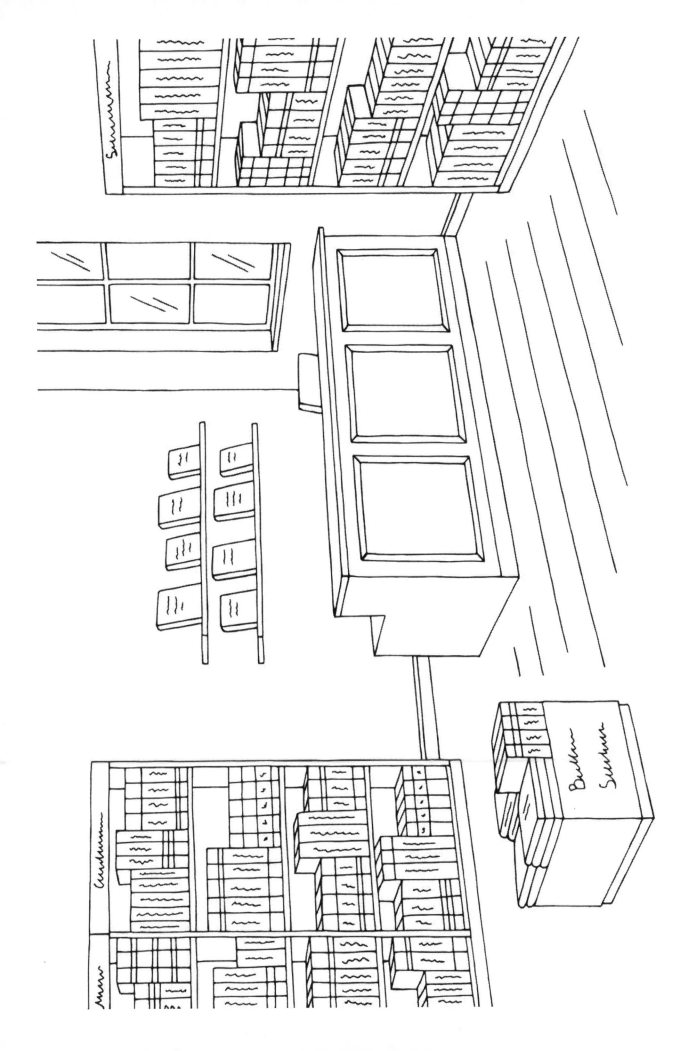

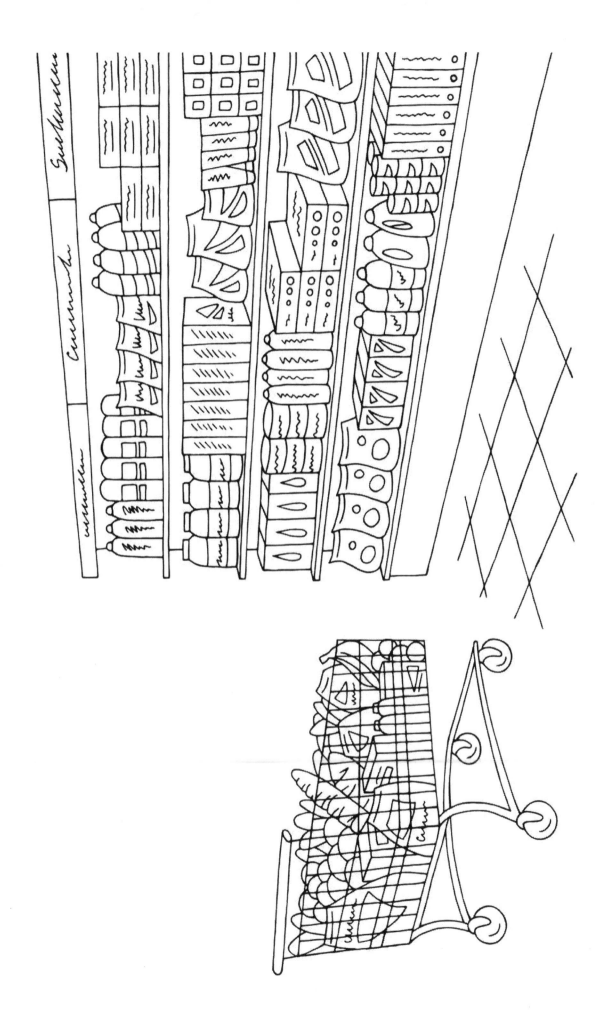

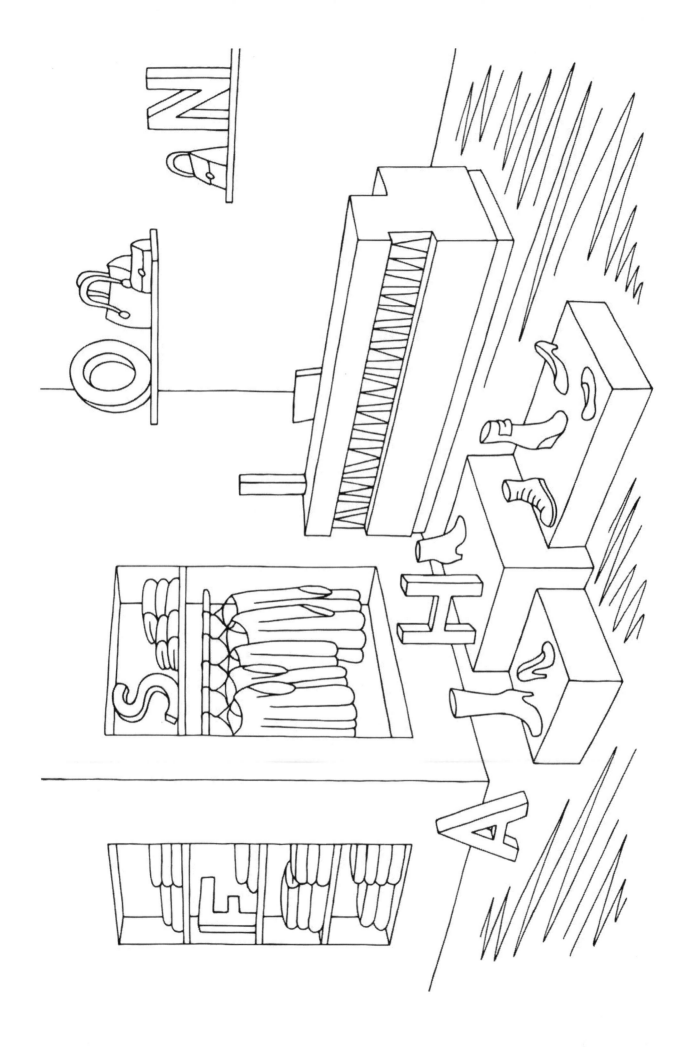

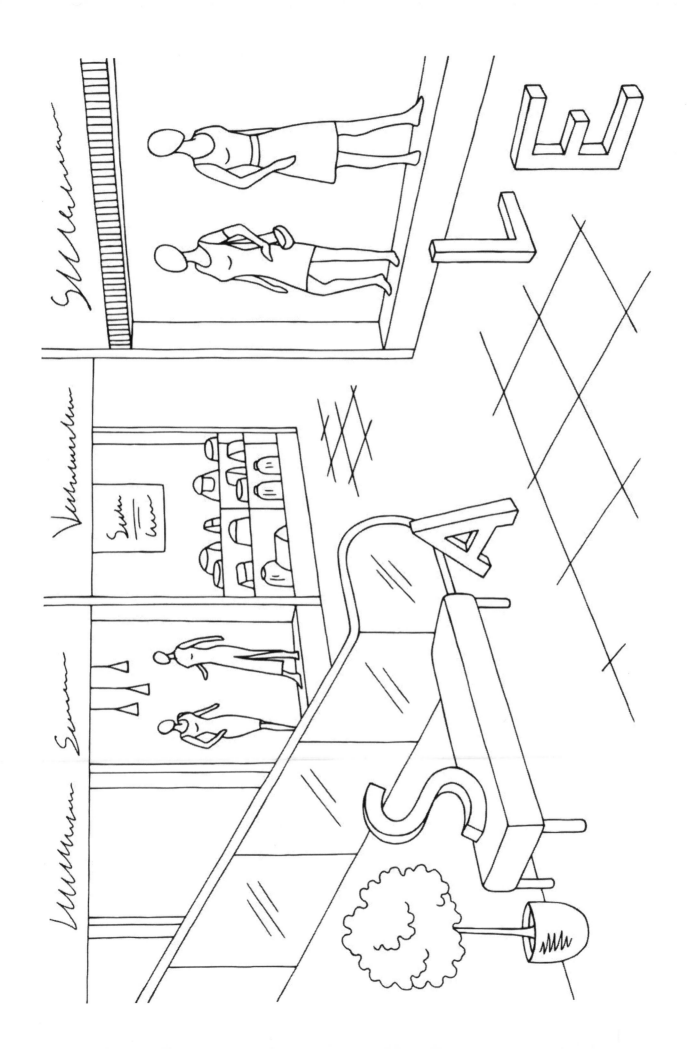

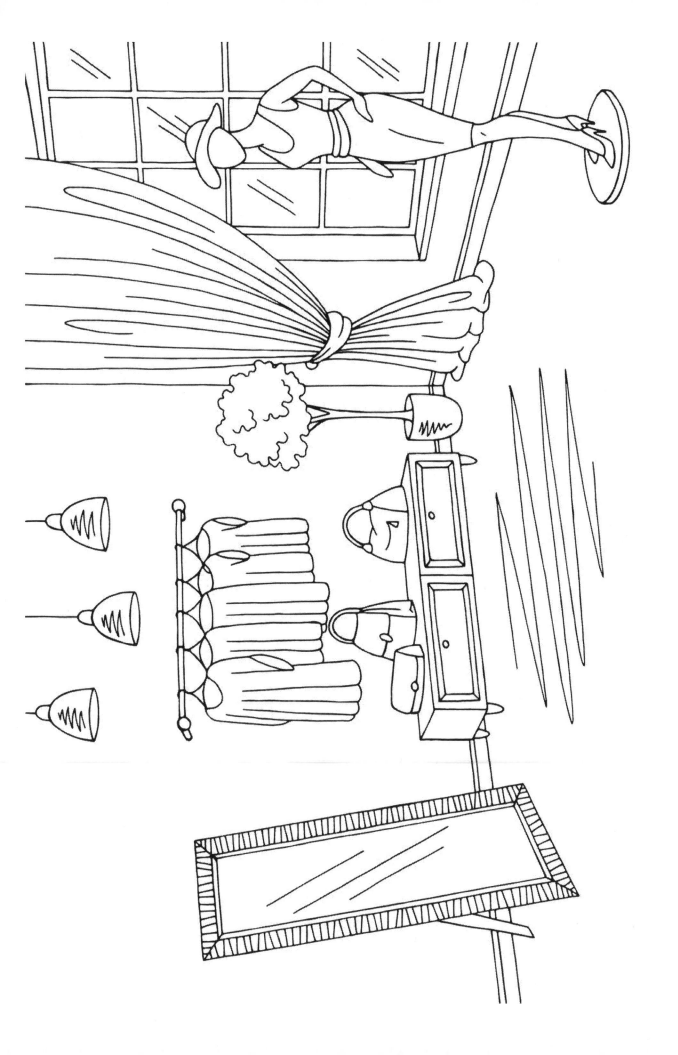

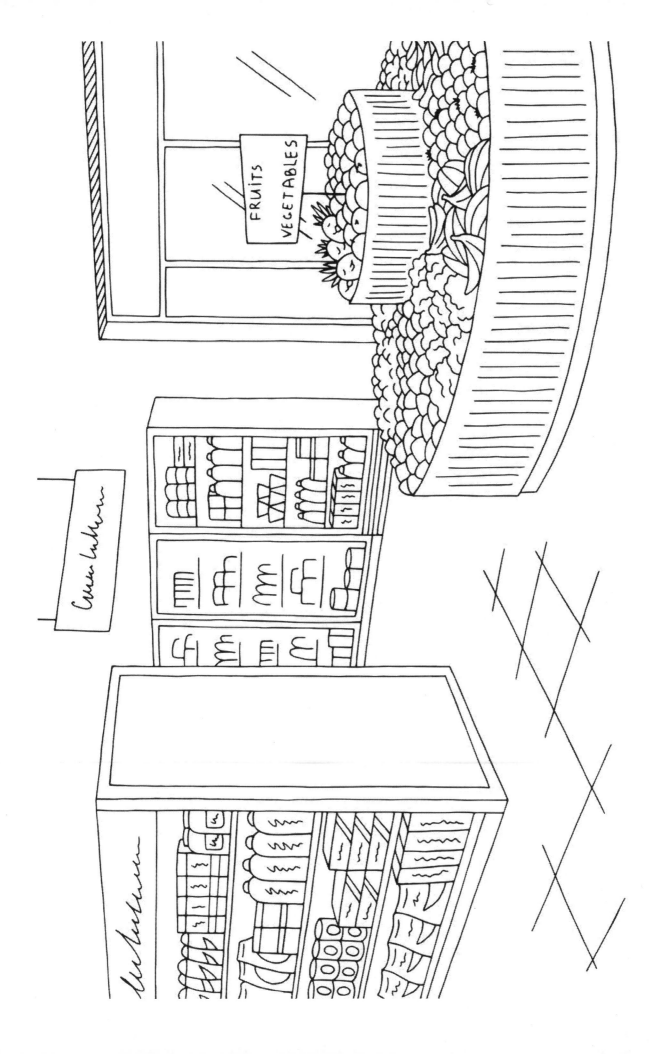

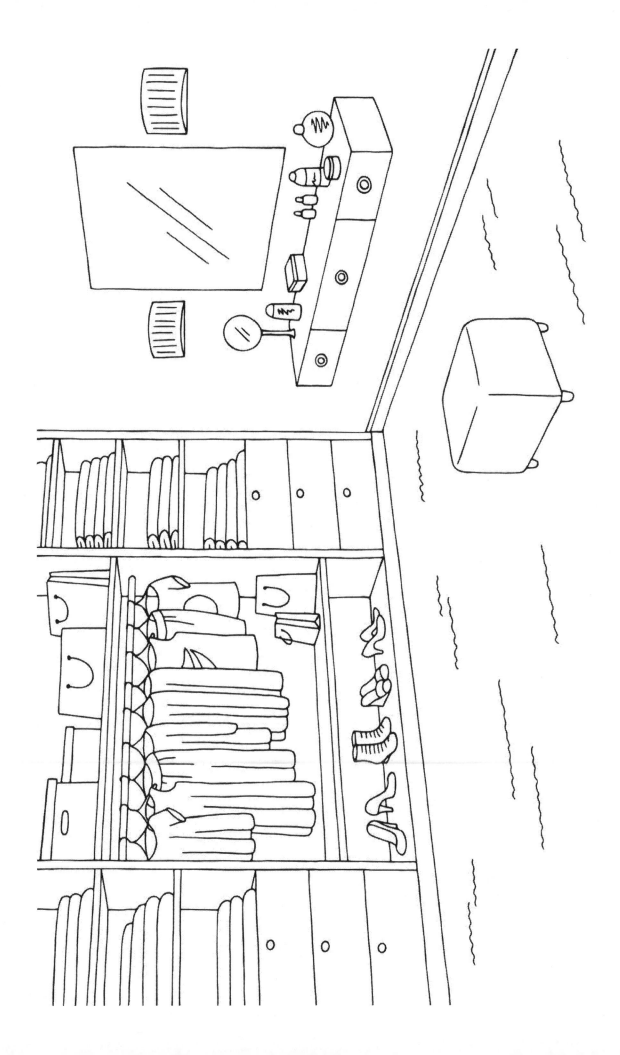

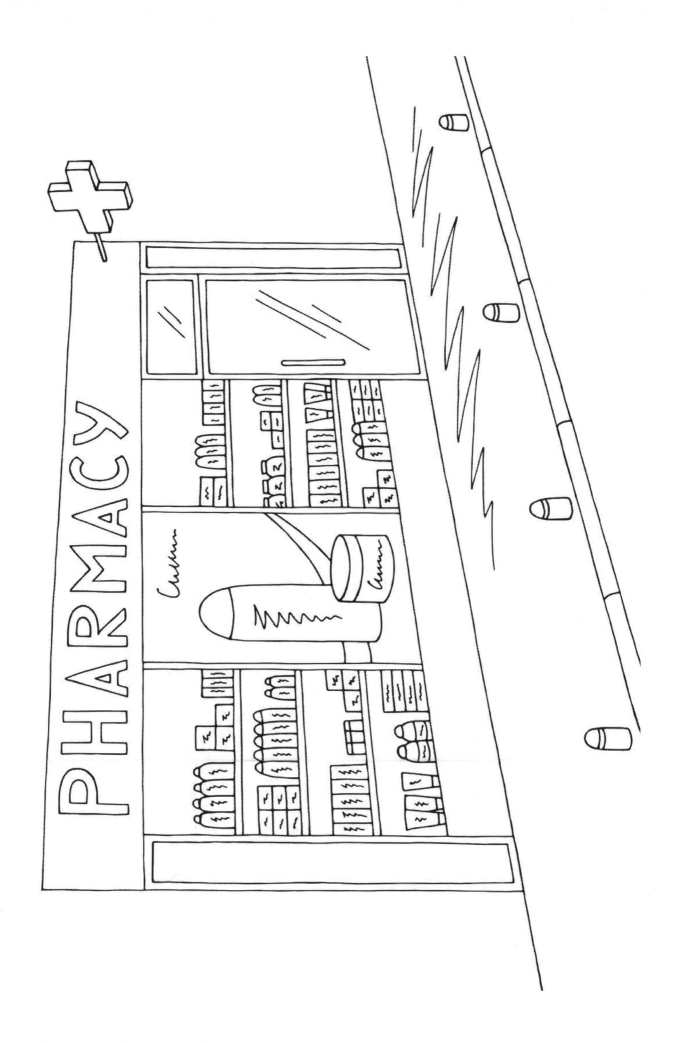

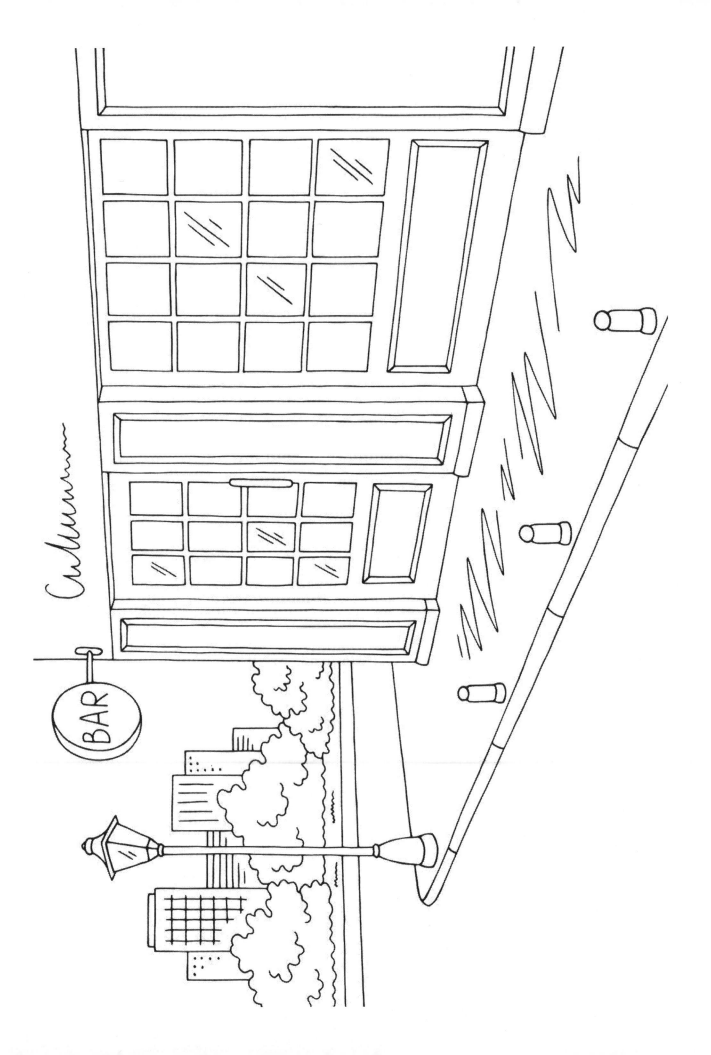

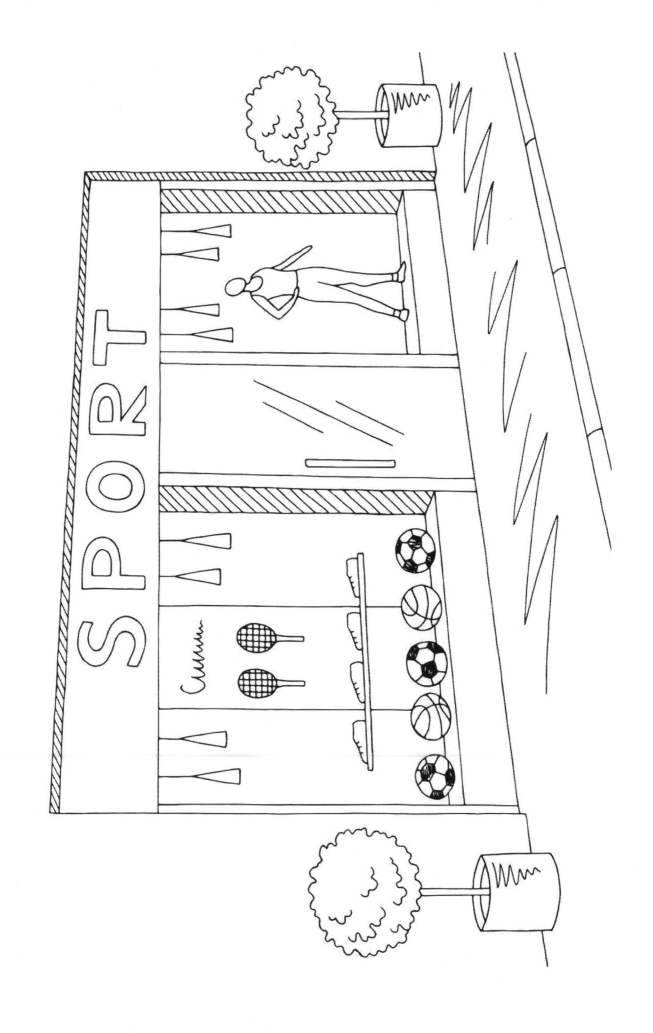

Thank you for coloring with us

Please consider to rate & review

More from our coloring books:

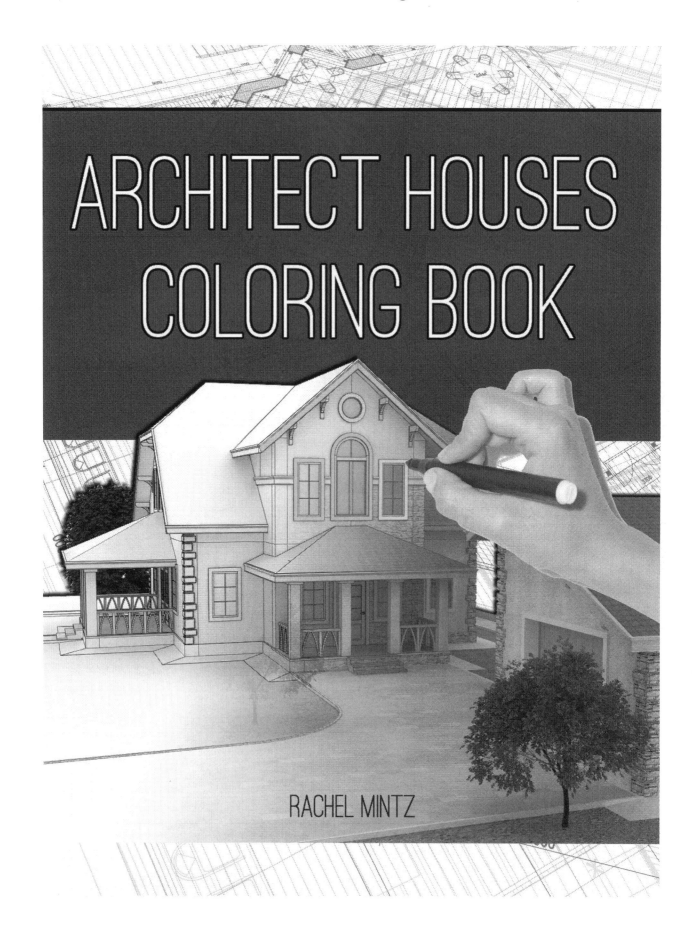

ARCHITECT HOUSES
COLORING BOOK

RACHEL MINTZ

ROOMS

INTERIOR DESIGN COLORING BOOK

RACHEL MINTZ

WONDERFUL AMSTERDAM

COLORING BOOK FOR ADULTS

RACHEL MINTZ

Join Our Coloring Books VIP Group
Members Get Giveaways, Deep Discount Offers,
Win Prizes – Visit Site To Join (It's Free)

www.ColoringBookHome.com

Thank you for coloring with us

Please consider to rate & review

Made in the USA
Monee, IL
19 March 2021